101
Innovative Ideas for Creative Kids

101 Innovative Ideas for Creative Kids

Claudia J. Dodson

CORWIN PRESS, INC.
A Sage Publications Company
Thousand Oaks, California

For information:

Corwin Press, Inc.
A Sage Publications Company
2455 Teller Road
Thousand Oaks, California 91320
E-mail: order@corwinpress.com

Sage Publications Ltd.
6 Bonhill Street
London EC2A 4PU
United Kingdom

Sage Publications India Pvt. Ltd.
M-32 Market
Greater Kailash I
New Delhi 110 048 India

Printed in the United States of America

Library of Congress Cataloging-in-Publication Data

Dodson, Claudia J.
101 innovative ideas for creative kids / by Claudia J. Dodson.
p.   cm.
Includes index.
ISBN 0-7619-7644-2 (cloth: alk. paper)
ISBN 0-7619-7645-0 (pbk.: alk. paper)
1. Education, Elementary—Activity programs.   2. Education,
Elementary—Curricula.   3. Creative activities and seat work.
I. Title: One hundred one innovative ideas for creative kids.
II. Title: One hundred and one innovative ideas for creative kids.
III. Title.
LB1592.D63   2000
372.5—dc21   00-008085

This book is printed on acid-free paper.

00   01   02   03   04   05   10   9   8   7   6   5   4   3   2   1

Corwin Editorial Assistant:	Julia Parnell
Production Editor:	Denise Santoyo
Editorial Assistant:	Victoria Cheng
Typesetter/Designer:	Janelle LeMaster

Contents

7. Fun Activities for Outdoor or Active Play   71

(All activities in Chapter 7 could be used to meet standards in
physical education, oral communication, or teamwork. Have fun, too!)

8. Motivational and Organizational Ideas   87

Preface

Because children are continually bombarded with a variety of media and technology, there is a need in education to present learning activities in new, different, and stimulating ways. Educators *will* keep interest and excitement toward learning with a daily search for new methods to present the ever growing information that children need to be successful in life. We can expect to be successful educators through reinventing ourselves professionally.

101 Innovative Ideas for Creative Kids is a ready reference for kindergarten through fifth-grade teachers who need ideas to invigorate their daily lessons in many areas of the elementary curriculum. The book also will be valuable for home school teachers and school-age (after-school) programs. Each activity can easily be adjusted to be appropriate for the grade level that is being taught. The activities are all self-explanatory and extremely easy to prepare. Because teachers struggle daily with time constraints, ease of preparation is a valuable characteristic of the ideas in this book.

The book is unique in style compared with most teacher idea books. Most books that are available have lots of work sheets to duplicate for student drill and practice. This book gives alternatives to the typical paper drill-and-practice approach. Children are more responsive to this book's interactive approach to learning. Once the concept is employed, the paper-and-pencil activities can easily be added as one assessment tool. This book includes ideas for seasonal projects, student motivation, class celebrations, and organization—definitely areas that teachers struggle with regularly. In addition, most teachers are expected to cover specific district, state, and even national education standards. To help teachers when planning lessons, I have noted, where applicable, the national education standard that could be met with specific activities.

101 Innovative Ideas for Creative Kids is organized into eight areas for which teachers are responsible throughout the year. In each chapter, there are seven or more practical, easy-to-implement, unique, and fun ideas.

The areas included are

1. Reading and Language Arts
2. Journal Writing Ideas
3. Class Books to Create
4. Mathematics
5. Science and Social Studies
6. Seasonal Ideas
7. Fun Activities for Outdoor or Active Play
8. Motivational and Organizational Ideas

I wrote this book for two reasons. First, I like the idea that someday my grandchildren or other future relatives might find a copy of my book and come to realize that I had positively affected a lot of children and had been well respected in my field. I strongly believe that teaching is one of the most important professions in the world. Second, I am optimistic that the unique and worthwhile ideas in my book will help other dedicated teachers who are scrambling to be everything to everyone with minimal time, help, and money. I know that when I help teachers, the students will end up having their education enhanced. I will be flattered and pleased if this book becomes valuable to hardworking educators and puts a smile on all children's faces.

Acknowledgments

The contributions of the following reviewers are gratefully acknowledged:

Beth Nason Quick
Director of Early Childhood Education, Tennessee State University
Nashville, Tennessee

Michelle Barnea
Educational Consultant
Rockaway, New Jersey

The contribution of my artist, Susan Schutte, is gratefully acknowledged. Susan is a busy art teacher, mother to a one-year-old son, and wife to another great educator. She was willing to take time from her busy life to draw great little pictures that should help my ideas come to life. Thanks go to her.

—Claudia J. Dodson

About the Author

CLAUDIA J. DODSON has been involved in education as teacher, deaf interpreter, math specialist, and librarian for more than 15 years and has collected great, workable ideas during that time. *101 Innovative Ideas for Creative Kids* is her first published work. Born and raised on a cattle ranch in Montana, she knew early on that she wanted to be a teacher. She graduated magna cum laude from Montana State University in 1980. She has taught in Pennsylvania, Montana, and Virginia and is currently a second-grade teacher in Chesapeake, Virginia. Although teaching is very important to her, her first love is her family. She is the proud parent of Tara (age 13) and Carter (age 8) and is married to a wonderful man named Bill. Her family has provided much love and support while she has ventured into the challenges of book publishing.

Summary of
National Education Standards

Reading and Language Arts Standards

1. Reading texts to understand culture
2. Reading texts to understand human experience
3. Comprehending and evaluating texts
4. Communicating for purpose and audience
5. Using writing process elements
6. Applying knowledge to create and create texts
7. Conducting research
8. Using technological and informational resources
9. Respecting diversity of language use
10. Using English as a second language
11. Participating in literary communities
12. Using language for personal purposes

National Council of Teachers of Mathematics Standards

1. Math as problem solving
2. Math as communication
3. Math as reasoning
4. Mathematical connections
5. Estimation
6. Number sense and numeration
7. Concepts of whole number operations
8. Whole number computation
9. Geometry and spatial sense
10. Measurement
11. Statistics and probability
12. Fractions and decimals
13. Patterns and relationships

National Council for Social Studies Standards

1. Culture
2. Time, continuity, and change
3. People, places, and environment
4. Individual identity and development
5. Individuals, groups, and institutions
6. Power, authority, and governance
7. Production, distribution, and consumption
8. Science, technology, and society
9. Global connections
10. Civic ideals and practices

National Science Education Standards

1. Science as inquiry
2. Physical science
3. Life science
4. Earth and space science
5. Science and technology
6. Science in personal and social perspectives
7. History and nature of science

1
Reading and Language Arts

All the ideas in Chapter 1, and throughout the book, can easily be adapted for kindergarten through fifth grade. The ideas allow the children to move around, work with partners, be creative, and most important, be engaged in the learning process. The more children are encouraged to do this, the more they *and you* will enjoy the process.

This first chapter contains ideas that reinforce concepts such as research skills, punctuation, parts of speech, types of writing, oral language development, genre study, word structure, and more. Each activity requires little preparation, but the results will be important to the children. When the work goes home, the parents will have a clear (and positive) picture of what is going on in their children's education.

1. Dictionary of the Class (L.A. #7)

Materials needed: Student photos, lined paper, and construction paper.

This project is a great way to review dictionary skills while creating a class dictionary. Have each child create an entry for him- or herself, with first and last names, part of speech (noun), definitions, picture (drawn or school photo), and sample sentence.

Example: Smith, Susan (n.) 1. A young woman, age 7, who goes to Shepherd Primary School. 2. A stamp collector and ballet lover. 3. The youngest child in the Smith Family. *(Susan Smith is a very helpful student.)*

Bind the pages alphabetically into a "Class Dictionary" that each child will take home.

John Jenson (noun): boy; brown hair; blue eyes; athlete.

2. Environmental Print Search (L.A. #2)

Materials needed: Various posters, signs, students' work, paper, and pencils.

Each week, form groups of two to three students and have the groups search around the room and/or school for examples of the language skill that they've been studying.

Examples: Long vowel/silent *e* words; words with common prefixes or suffixes; *ch, sh, th,* and *wh* words; *thr, spr,* and *str* words; nouns; contractions; and so forth.

Places to search include the classroom, hallway, student books, or any place that the printed words can be found. To keep work organized, have each group fold their paper in fourths or eighths, depending on how many categories they're searching for. Have children label each section with the category.

A quarter-long contest could be held to see who is most successful searching for all the categories of words. You could offer some sort of prize to encourage careful searching.

3. Class Quilt (L.A. #12)

Materials needed: Outline shapes, inkpad, markers, and paper.

Save old die-cutting machine outline pieces and join enough for one per student. If the pieces are joined in configurations such as five rows of five, the result will resemble a quilt of apples, bears, schoolhouses, or whatever outline shapes you choose. You need one shape per student, plus you could have extra shapes mixed in that tell about the class. Use white paper as a backing, and have each child put a fingerprint (using an inkpad) in the middle of his or her quilt piece. Have the children add hair, legs, arms, clothing, and so forth to their fingerprint "heads" and put their names at the bottom of their creations.

In addition to the quilt, have each child write a short essay that describes her- or himself, including information such as age, family data, and favorite hobbies. Number the essays, and see if children and adults can match the picture with the essay. This makes a wonderful decoration for use during open house.

4. Noodle Quotes (L.A. #3)

Materials needed: Paper, glue, and elbow pasta noodles.

When you introduce quotation marks to your class, the use of elbow pasta noodles provides a good visual reminder. Work together to create examples of conversation that need quotation marks, leaving out the actual words spoken.

Example: "_____!" screamed the young child. "_____," explained the nice teacher.

Give the students a supply of noodles and have them complete the examples with "noodle quotes" and words they think would have been spoken in the situation. Remind them that quotes always "hug" the words spoken in sentences. Another good reinforcement of quotation marks is to have the children use their index and middle fingers of both hands as visual quotation marks when they are reading orally.

5. Folktale News (L.A. #9)

Materials needed: Books of folktales, paper, and pencils.

A way to emphasize the Who, What, Where, When, and Why questions is using folktales. This activity also provides a way to check for understanding of literature read. Have each child choose a tale to adapt into an article for a "Fairy Tale Adventures" newspaper.

Example: Small Girl Busts Bears' Furniture

Deep in the Forest—Yesterday, the police received a report from Mama, Papa, and Baby Bear that numerous pieces of furniture in their small home had been busted. They called the police after coming home to shattered chairs and food missing from their breakfast table. They believe a small blonde child might be involved in this vandalism. When they were checking upstairs for more damage, they found the child asleep. When she awoke, she appeared very startled and dashed from the home. No arrests have yet been made in this case. If you have information, call Crime Line at (757) 555-4310.

6. Word Ending/Beginning Flip Book (L.A. #5)

Materials needed: Sentence strip paper and pencils.

To help teach word endings and beginnings, give each child six to eight pieces of sentence strip paper approximately 6 inches long and one piece 7 inches long. On the longer paper, write *es, ing, ed,* or another ending right at the end of the strip. You could also put letters such as *sh, ch, str,* and so forth at the beginning of the longer strip. On the other papers, write words that use the ending or blend.

> **Example:** *es: beaches, bushes, catches, fishes, wishes; sh: shop, shirt, shelly, shoe, shoshone*

This activity is good for rule review. Write the ending/blend on the bottom, punch holes in all cards, add yarn to hold cards together, and the children will have their personal "Flip Books" to study from. These books are quite effective for home review when children are struggling with reading skills. They also will improve the spelling of the words when the children can see the "parts" that make words.

7. Cartoon Sequencing (L.A. #1)

Materials needed: Cartoons collected from newspapers, scissors, and tagboard.

To provide good practice with sequencing skills, take cartoons from the newspaper that will appeal to children and cut them into the individual frames. Mount the frames on tagboard to make small cards. Give them to groups of children to discuss and place in the correct order. Use some sort of code on the back for self-correcting. At times, children will put them in an order other than what the cartoonist intended. If they can make a logical justification for that order, that's perfectly acceptable.

An additional idea related to this activity is to have the children create their own cartoons, cut them apart, and see if their classmates can figure out the order. This activity offers an opportunity for artistic expression, encourages children to be creative thinkers, and may reveal those students who can create humor.

8. Around the Room Recording (L.A. #11)

Materials needed: Tape recorder, book, and audiotape.

Take a story that all students can read with confidence, and divide it up into paragraphs. Give each child a paragraph and record the entire story by having a different child read each paragraph. Stop the recorder after each child. Get the next one ready, push record, wait 2 seconds, and you're ready for the next student. This activity is good for assessing oral reading skills, is super to share at open house celebrations, and is a visual way to teach about paragraphs. (The students will soon be able to spot where the story is "dented in" and also quickly find the main idea.)

Later, once the children are comfortable with having their voices recorded, find folktales and ethnic stories that the children will enjoy. See if the children can read with an accent or dialect while you work with them on expressive reading. This will easily reveal the children with hidden theatrical talent.

9. Rhyming Relay (L.A. #4)

Materials needed: 30+ index cards labeled with the word endings listed below.

This activity reinforces rhyming patterns and sight vocabulary. Before starting, prepare index cards similar to the following: *unk, an, ig, up, ow, ack, aw, ide, oat, ight, est, ay, ain, ick, or, ap,* and so on. Divide the class into two groups. As you hold up a card, the first member of each team tries to create a word.

Example: *unk: trunk, bunk, chunk, skunk, junk*

Continue the play as long as the children can come up with different words using that ending. When neither team can make a rhyming word, a point is rewarded to the team that made the last word. Play continues with all the other word ending cards. An extension of this activity is for the students to pick a few endings and make a list of all the words they can think of. This activity can also be the start of a poetry unit as you introduce poetry with ending rhyme and free verse.

10. Totally Terrific Tongue Twisters (L.A. #12)

Materials needed: Paper, pencils, and art supplies.

A fun way to reinforce the idea of alliteration is by having each child pick a letter sound and write a tongue twister that uses that sound predominantly. This is also a perfect chance to show that different letters can make a similar sound.

Examples: *Eigh:* long A, *A-E:* long A: Eighty-eight angry ants ate all the apples at the A&P.
C and S sound like *sssss:* Six slimy snakes slithered through the salty swamp in Sandbridge this century.

Once the tongue twister is written, have children illustrate their writing. A contest could be held for the best tongue twister reader. Bind all the creations into a book to be shared with parents.

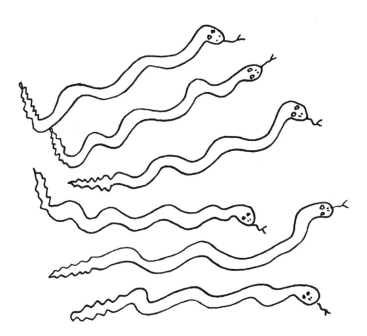

11. Pick a Part of Speech (L.A. #3)

Materials needed: 25+ index cards with words similar to the ones listed below, each category written in different colors for easy separation.

This activity is great for showing the role of nouns, adjectives, adverbs, and so on in sentences. Prior to the activity, create an envelope with numerous examples of the parts of speech, such as these:

Plural nouns: *Barbies, monsters, desks*

Verbs: *ran, yelled, slept*

Adjectives (number words): *five, a million, many*

Adjectives (color words): *red, violet, colorful*

Adjectives (size words): *huge, tiny, skinny*

Adjectives (texture words): *hairy, smooth, fluffy*

Adjectives (feeling words): *angry, nice, scared*

Adverbs: *now, later, in the house*

Have each child pick one word from each of the noun, verb, and adverb categories and two words from the adjective categories. In addition, *a, an,* and *the* may be needed. Display each "crazy" sentence on a sentence strip. The children will love all the combinations possible.

adj.   adj.   n.   v.   adv.
"Crazy" Sentence Example: The skinny hairy Barbies yelled in the house!

2

Journal Writing Ideas

Writing in a journal is one of the best ways for children to become more fluent and confident writers. Possible journal topics (Ideas 12-44) are shown in this chapter. Children need to feel free to write their own ideas, whatever they may be, and should not be limited to only the vocabulary with which they are completely comfortable. If you do little editing of journals and, for the most part, just add short personal comments and a few suggestions to the students' ideas, students will be encouraged to continue writing. Because parents may not appreciate unedited work, attach the letter at the end of this section (see Figure 2.1) to each child's journal to limit concerns. At the beginning of the year, it is wise to set up a standard format for class journal writing. Putting the date and topic at the top of the paper is a good habit to instill early. Using margins and checking punctuation, capitalization, and obvious spelling errors will also become habitual if you keep them part of the process each time that students write. Most children need to be taught a system of neatness or organization—they will thank you later!

12 to 44. Writing Starters (L.A. #5)

Materials needed for Ideas 12 to 44: Paper, pencils, and imagination.

One place I have fun is _____. I like it because . . .

Five terrific after-school snacks are
(1) _____, (2) _____, (3) _____, (4) _____, (5) _____.

One time that I spent the night away from my family was . . .

If there was a new baby in my family, I . . .

My favorite outfit is . . .

The best thing about winter (spring, summer, fall) is . . .

Other reasons that I like _____ are . . .

The ten best things about school are
(1) _____, (2) _____ , (3) _____, and so forth.

I opened the giant treasure chest and . . . (story starter)

The rules for playing football (baseball, basketball, rummy, etc.) are
(1)_____, (2)_____, (3)_____, and so on.

Here are the things I know about fire safety!

A game I enjoy is . . . The way you play is . . .

The costume party was . . . (story starter)

My father (mother) is . . . He (she) likes to . . . His (her) job is . . .

If I were teaching _____, I would . . .

My favorite part of recess is . . .

Something I am good at is . . .

Some jobs I have at home are . . . My favorite is . . . because . . .

The most perfect day I can think of would be . . .

During the holiday break, I will . . .

One famous person I know about is . . . He (she) became famous because . . .

Some important things I have learned in _____ grade are . . .

My favorite nutritious meal is . . .

Ten years from now, in the year _____, I will . . .

If a genie granted me three wishes, I would . . .

One time that I felt very sad/happy/lonely was . . .

My favorite book is . . . It is about . . .

The best thing about a rainy/snowy/windy day is . . .

I have really changed since I was six. Then, I . . . Now, I . . . have important jobs.

They . . . I had good reason to feel . . . First, . . . (story starter)

If I were a parent, I would . . .

In the year 2040, computers will . . .

 A favorite memory from this year was when . . .

Figure 2.1. Sample Parent Letter

Dear Parents:

This journal will be used all year by your child to improve writing skills and share unique ideas. Twice a week, a topic will be placed on the board to stimulate thought and improve writing. Your child's personal thoughts and opinions will be written, so this journal is really quite similar to a diary.

Because of the personal nature of journal writing, I will make comments only about the subject matter of the entries and a few suggestions on how to improve punctuation, spelling, grammar, and so forth. (With more editing, the children tend to get discouraged, and the writing suffers.)

After each quarter, I will send the journal home for you to enjoy. Please spend time with your child reading selected entries. I'm sure that your child will enjoy this time with you and will learn from your suggestions for improvement.

Sincerely,

Your Child's Teacher

3

Class Books to Create

All the ideas in this section can easily be bound into books using binding machines or staples or by doing a simple sewing stitch with a sewing machine down the center of each book. Having a collection of work by all the students in the class together in one book provides a valuable opportunity to assess individual differences, abilities, and weaknesses visually. An added bonus is that the children will take pride in their part of each book and will enjoy reading and rereading books created during the year. A wonderful goal is to create enough classroom books so that at the end of the year, each child can receive one to take home and add to her or his personal library. Many children will cherish these books long after they move on and will use them as a means of remembering their classmates and teacher.

45. Book of Opposites (L.A. #6)

Materials needed for activities 45 through 52: All need only art paper and drawing supplies.

Pair children up and give them a piece of paper that has been folded in half. Each group draws and labels two sets of opposites.

Example: *Big/Little:* One child draws a big object and the other a small object.

Other opposites are a little more challenging, such as *happy/sad.* Bind papers in a book for the class to enjoy. An extension of this activity is an "Around the World" game: Have two students stand. Say one opposite and listen to see who will say the other the quickest. The winner keeps going "Around the World" until defeated. Analogies could also be introduced, such as *pretty* is to *ugly* as *black* is to _____, *finger* is to *arm* as *tire* is to _____, *teeth* is to *chew* as *ear* is to _____, and *glove* is to *hand* as *shoe* is to _____.

46. Book of Comparatives (L.A. #6)

This activity will pleasantly reinforce the idea of comparisons using *er* and *est*. Divide a paper in thirds and label with words such as *nice, nicer,* and *nicest.* Have the children illustrate the comparatives. A class activity that children enjoy is to group the students in threes and have them line up according to big, bigger, and biggest, or, conversely, small, smaller, and smallest. As a group, they could write sentences describing their comparisons. Eventually, the whole class could be compared until you have located the biggest to the smallest (by height, of course). Other examples include *pretty, prettier, prettiest; silly, sillier, silliest;* and *hungry, hungrier, hungriest.* This is the perfect time to discuss the rules for dropping *e,* changing *y* to *i,* and doubling consonants. Once again, children will be likely to look their work over and refresh their learning if the papers are bound into a class book.

47. Book of 1,000 (M. #6)

A fun way to teach about larger numbers and celebrate the 100th day of the year is to assign groups of two or three children to draw 100 of any one item or one category of items. Examples include pencils, balloons, students, birds, planets, crayons, and so on. Have 10 groups each draw 100 objects, and bind the 10 pages into a book of 1,000. Another possible way to accomplish this is to have students cut objects from magazines. Examples include 100 vowels, names of people, faces, and so forth. Children will be fascinated with the finished books, and at least a few will try to count all 1,000 items. This can be a great opportunity to work on place value and four-digit numbers.

Another good illustration of 1,000 is to take ten 100s place value blocks and tie them together to make one big cube that illustrates 1,000. This will help children gradually internalize the concept that our numbering system is based on values of 10 (10 ones = 1 ten, 10 tens = 1 hundred, 10 hundreds = 1 thousand).

48. Class How-to Book (L.A. #4)

Divide the class into four to six groups. Have each group pick a simple task with which they are familiar. Groups will write the directions for the task as clearly as possible. They need to use direction words such as *first, then, after that, next,* and *finally.* The group will also need to make illustrations to accompany the directions. Some possible topics are how to carve a pumpkin, how to make the bed, how to build a snowman, or how to make a peanut butter and jelly sandwich.

An extension of this activity is for each group to critique another group's directions to see if any vital information is missing. To illustrate the need for clear instructions, bring in the ingredients and tools needed to create peanut butter and jelly sandwiches and have a volunteer or two follow *exactly* the instructions that have been written to see how things turn out. Also, the children could take turns taking the book home to try out the directions on one or more of the tasks described.

49. Our Book of Birthdays (S.S. #2)

This activity is a good one to use to reinforce calendar skills and learn about classmates. Have each child create a page of the book with these sentences on the bottom:

My birthday is on _____.

On my last birthday, I turned _____ years old.

On my next birthday, I want to celebrate by _____.

When children celebrate their birthdays, have them show their pages. At the top of each page will be the child's name along with a "birthday picture." The book should be organized by month and day within the month. This book provides a good opportunity for teaching capitalization of proper nouns, abbreviation of months, the number of days in each month, and the spelling of the months. This can also be a good chance to discuss birth years.

Example: If you were born in 1996, how old will you be in the year 2005?
(Four-digit subtractions will result: 2005 – 1996 = 9.)

In addition, the birth dates of famous people could be discussed—for example, Abraham Lincoln, Christopher Columbus, and Susan B. Anthony.

50. Looking Into the Future (S.S. #4)

During career week or during any occupation studies, this activity will fit in and be fun. Have all children create a two-part page for a class book. On one half, have them write "What I Can Do Now." In this section, children illustrate something they are proud of doing now. On the other half, have students write "And in 20 Years, I Will . . ." In this section, have them draw themselves as adults doing what they hope to do. (This is also a good opportunity to practice adding dates: In 20 years, what will the date be?)

Once the class book is finished, various extensions of this activity are possible. For example, have students find books on the careers chosen for the future and do a little research on the education, responsibilities, and opportunities for those careers. In addition, an economic discussion on salaries, taxes, benefits, and so on could fit right in. For a homework assignment, have children interview their parents about what they wanted to be when they were children and compare those goals with what they've actually ended up doing. Interesting . . .

51. Compound Creations (L.A. #3)

The study of compounds is always fun, but this book may bring an extra giggle to the day. Give each child a paper that has been folded in half. Have the children choose two compounds to illustrate. Some possibilities are butter + fly = butterfly (pat of butter and a fly?). Others that work well include *rainbow, snowman,* and *blackout.* After the book is created, have the children take a part from the front of one compound and a part from the back of another and create new compounds such as *butterbow* or *rainfly.* Have children explain what they are and how they might be used. A story-writing assignment challenge could be issued to see who can use the most compounds (logically) in a story. This is another opportunity to play the "Around the World" game as described in Idea 45.

52. Holiday Book for 20— (S.S. #3)

Shortly after winter break, this activity is a great one to introduce the new year. Have the children list on the board the major holidays for the year, such as Halloween, Easter, Christmas, and Veteran's Day. Try to get at least one for each month. Have the class study a large calendar and figure out the date for each holiday for the present year. Have each child choose a holiday to illustrate and label as follows:

Example: Labor Day in 2000 will be on September 4. It will be on the first Monday of the month. On Labor Day, I will probably . . .

This activity helps with calendar skills and holiday recognition (proper nouns) and is a good introduction to collecting "Favorite Holiday" data for bar graph work. The finished work should be bound chronologically for another fun class book to share.

4

Mathematics

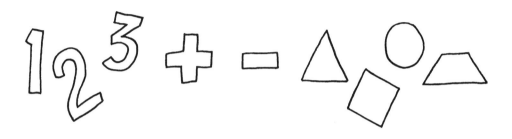

All the math ideas in this chapter involve active participation by the children. These learning activities are valuable to use when introducing new concepts and also when revisiting old concepts. When children "see" how numbers work, they will then have a true understanding that will stick with them. In addition, many of the activities relate math to real-life experiences, for example, "Pizza Fractions" and "Measurement Olympics." Children frequently view math as abstract concepts that have little to do with day-to-day life. When they realize that math is used in many situations in their lives, math becomes more valuable to them. Also, when children "play" during math time, it becomes something to look forward to, instead of dreading. Fun is one of the best approaches available to teachers!

53. Dice Game (M. #6)

Materials needed: Two dice per group, paper, and pencils.

Group students in sets of two to four. Each player takes turns tossing the dice and adding the total from both dice. The score the player gets is the total for that round. Each score is added to the one from the previous round. The game is over when players reach a predetermined score, such as 100. (This game can be used for subtraction or multiplication as well.) The game will ensure that you are getting in basic computation drill time without the moans and groans.

As a challenge, students can attempt to get to exactly 100 (or some other chosen number) points. When they get to 90+ and can't get that magical sum or difference, the excitement will go up. Another possibility is to take the winner from each group and have a tournament to see who is the "Dice Math" Champ. Group winners for round one and then take those winners until you are down to one champ.

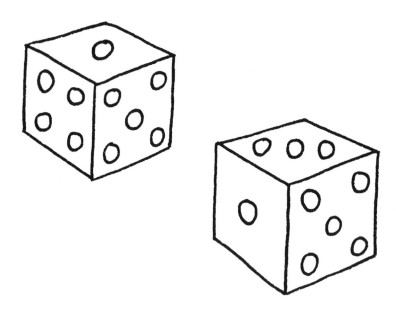

54. I'm Thinking of a Number (M. #5)

Materials needed: None.

Choose a number in your head and then say, "I'm thinking of a number." The students take turns asking yes or no questions.

Examples: Is it even? Is it above 50? Is it in the 30s?

The children need to keep track of the clues in their heads. When the clues have narrowed the number possibilities down, announce that it's time for guesses. The student who guesses the number correctly receives a small prize. This activity is good for mental math, memory, and logic skills. This activity will, if nothing else, get the children to recognize odd numbers (ending in 1, 3, 5, 7, or 9) and even numbers (ending in 0, 2, 4, 6, or 8). Another way to teach that concept is to say large numbers and call on students to identify the numbers as odd or even.

Example: 2, 187, 311: Ends in a one—it's odd!

55. Bingo Math (M. #6)

Materials needed: Bingo cards, dried beans for markers, and pencils.

Give each student a blank bingo card (5 rows with 5 squares per row). Have students write in numbers between 1 and 75. To play the game, provide the students with bean "markers" and then give them problems to add or subtract, for example, $21 + 16$ or $85 - 74$. A student with that answer puts a marker on it. When a student has a row—horizontally, vertically, diagonally, or four corners—the student calls out "Bingo!" This activity is great for increasing speed of basic computation while maintaining students' enthusiasm. Another possibility is to have the children create the cards and then swap them with classmates so that they are not creating problems that they can easily solve. Bingo math may also be used for multiplication and division problems.

BINGO	MATH			
1	44	6	3	13
30	29	17	25	2
63	72	50	15	12
8	36	11	9	16
75	14	7	20	100

56. Measurement Olympics (M. #10)

Materials needed: Work sheet (see Figure 4.1), scales, marbles, cotton balls, straws, paper plates, rulers, yardsticks, sponge, water container, small box, and pennies.

This idea is designed as a culminating activity of a measurement unit. The children are given a sheet listing the "Olympic Events" in which they first estimate what they think the distance, weight, and volume for each event will be. They then rotate among the various stations and measure to see how close they are to their estimates. Possible events include Paper Plate Throw (distance), One-Handed Marble Grab (weight), Sponge Squeeze (liquid measurement), Cotton Ball Putt (distance), Straw Javelin (distance), and Penny Box Fill (volume). The child with the most accurate estimates is the gold medalist. Standard and/or metric units may be used. The children will have great fun with this and will see real examples of measurement. Warning: Undoubtedly, the noise level will be high!

Figure 4.1. Measurement Olympics Work Sheet

Name of competitor _____

Event	Estimated Measurement	Actual Measurement
Paper Plate Throw	_____ meters	_____ meters
	_____ yards	_____ yards
Marble Grab		
	_____ ounces	_____ ounces
	_____ grams	_____ grams
Sponge Squeeze		
	_____ cups	_____ cups
	_____ milliliters	_____ milliliters
Cotton Ball Putt		
	_____ inches	_____ inches
	_____ centimeters	_____ centimeters
Straw Javelin		
	_____ decimeters	_____ decimeters
	_____ feet	_____ feet
Penny Box Fill		
	_____ Numbers to fill	_____ Numbers to fill
	_____ Length, width, & height of box	_____ Length, width, & height of box

57. Money Practice Fun (M. #4)

Materials needed: Chalkboard, chalk, paper, and pencils.

A quick, easy way to have children practice counting money is to assign letter symbols for each coin, for example, P for penny, N for nickel, D for dime, Q for quarter, and F for 50-cent piece (half dollar). Write problems on the chalkboard using the letters (such as QQQDDNP = ?) or write money amounts (such as $1.05) and have children come up with combinations that equal that amount ($1.05 = QQQQN, DDDDDFPPPPP, or NNNDQQNQ, for example). Another possibility is playing "Around the World" (see Idea 45). For example, use the letters DDPPPPQ and have the children come up with the answer ($0.49) quickly. These activities are an excellent way for children to see that there are many correct ways to count money. Charts such as Ways to Make a Dollar can be added to daily.

Ways to Make a Dollar

	Pennies	Nickels	Dimes	Quarters	Half Dollars
Exp.	5	8	3	1	

58. Symmetry/Reflection (M. #9)

Materials needed: Art paper, paint, and other drawing materials.

Give each child a piece of paper folded in half. Each child squeezes out a design on one half of the paper using squeeze bottles of paint or colored glue. The work needs to be quick so the paint doesn't dry. Once the design is created, the child presses the paper together and gently separates it. The resulting design will be symmetrical and opens opportunities for creative thought in trying to visualize objects in the designs. Marker or crayon additions may be put on once the paint is dry—identical on both sides, of course. For fun, start an "inkblot" game, in which children are asked what they see in each picture. A nature hike to look around the school for symmetrical objects would also be fun! ("Did you see that butterfly?") Another variation is to take pictures of symmetrical objects, cut them in half, hold them to a mirror, and notice how the "whole" reappears.

59. Pizza Fractions (M. #12)

Materials needed: Cardboard circles from pizzas, construction paper, and art supplies.

Providing visual illustrations for fractions is the best way to ensure true understanding of the concept. Take the cardboard circles that have been saved, and, using masking tape, divide the "pizzas" into halves, fourths, sixths, and so on. Have students draw, paint, or glue on the sauce, pepperoni, cheese, onions, and other toppings. If you place the "pizzas" on display, children can easily see that three sixths of a pizza is the same as one half (equivalent fractions). They can also see that one eighth is smaller than one third (numerator/denominator study). Also, if some pizzas have a few pieces missing, it will be clear that if two fifths of a pizza has been eaten, then three fifths still remains (addition and subtraction of fractions). An additional way to make fractions become real is to have an actual pizza, cake, or pie party and demonstrate why most of us would rather have one sixth, rather than one twelfth, of a pizza.

60. Visual Multiplication (M. #7)

Materials needed: Index cards, dried beans, glue, and pencils.

To show students what multiplication is all about, take index cards and dried beans and glue on sets equaling various multiplication problems.

Examples: 2×3 (two groups of three beans) and 3×2 (three groups of two beans)

Have the children use the cards to create thought problems.

Example: Suzie had two bowls of fruit, one with three apples and one with three kiwis. How many pieces of fruit did she have in all?

Many times, "seeing" is understanding. Another way to reinforce the concept of multiplication is when the children are skip counting. At an early age, children can count by twos, fives, and so on. When children count, have them, instead of just saying "5, 10, 15, say "one group of 5 is 5, 1×5; two groups of 5 are 10, 2×5); three groups of 5 are 15, 3×5," and so on. Another visual technique is to take a set of beans, such as 12 for each student. Have each student group them a different way, such as one set of 12, two sets of 6, three sets of 4, and so on.

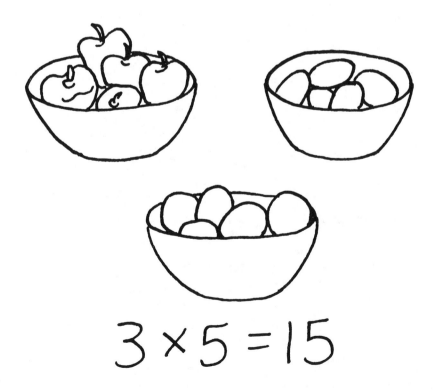

61. Hundreds Chart Math (M. #4)

Materials needed: Hundreds charts and a clear marker for each student.

Give each child a chart from 1 to 100 that shows the 10s in a vertical row: 10, 20, 30, and so on. If clear markers are not available, children can use their fingers. For example, say something such as, "Start at 22, go forward 3, subtract 6, add 10 [demonstrate going down one row for 10], take away 1, and what is your answer?" (29).

This activity increases speed of basic computation and reinforces understanding of adding 10s. You can also have the children give the directions for their classmates. The hundreds chart can also be used to reinforce skip counting. Put a code on the board such as this:

Example: Circle all even numbers. Put a square around those used when counting by 10s.
Draw a diagonal line through the 5s, and so on.

This will provide a quick visual check for understanding and also can show that numbers fit more than one criterion at times.

1	2	3	4	5	6	7	8	9	10
11	12	13	14	15	16	17	18	19	20
21	22	23	24	25	26	27	28	29	30
31	32	33	34	35	36	37	38	39	40
41	42	43	44	45	46	47	48	49	50
51	52	53	54	55	56	57	58	59	60
61	62	63	64	65	66	67	68	69	70
71	72	73	74	75	76	77	78	79	80
81	82	83	84	85	86	87	88	89	90
91	92	93	94	95	96	97	98	99	100

62. Great Graphs (M. #3)

Materials needed: Paper, pencils, and graph paper.

The following topics are easy for elementary children to graph:

Example: What is your favorite ice cream? Sport? Color? Fruit? Breakfast food? Type of
meat? School subject? Day of the week?

Other graphing ideas include eye colors, birthday month, and number of people in family. A fun activity is to host a graph afternoon. Group two to three students together and give each group one or two graph topics. Have each group interview their classmates and create a graph. Teach about tally marks for keeping track. Have each group come up with four or five possibilities to choose from for the answers, for example, favorite sport: baseball, football, dance, or wrestling. Challenge the groups to show their results in a creative way. (Draw a soccer ball, football, toe shoe, etc.) Be warned that there will be mass confusion when students are gathering data. At the end of the afternoon, have each group share their results and make plans for a future party to play the "favorite sport" or eat the "favorite ice cream."

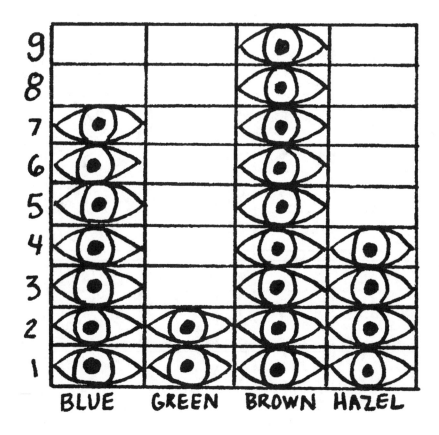

5

Science and Social Studies

Science and social studies are among the best areas of the curriculum to have fun with! The subject matter is perfect for class projects, hands-on creating, gung-ho researching, cooking, and more. Taking the time to organize the materials the first time will guarantee you years of purposeful and enjoyable learning activities that will help motivate even your least-inspired students. These projects require materials that parents can supply. In most instances, parents are glad to send in materials when they can see that their children are having a worthwhile educational experience. It is also good to get the parents into the classroom to actively help with the more involved projects that you are putting together. Seeing teaching in action most often builds great respect for the profession.

63. Magnetic Magic (S. #2)

Materials needed: Magnets of all shapes and sizes, iron filings, laminating film scraps, and tape.

Children will play for hours with a couple of magnets. With a little guidance, that play time can be very educational. In addition to everyday magnets that teachers have in school-supplied kits, iron filings, which can be acquired from brake installation shops (piles of filings are left behind from grinding of brakes), make great educational tools. Take about an eighth of a cup of the filings and secure filings inside two pieces of laminating film (tape the entire exterior). You then have a great educational tool to teach about fields of magnetic attraction. If you put a picture of a face under the filing package, children can manipulate the magnets to add "hair" and "mustaches" to the face.

Another fun activity for teaching about the poles of the magnet is to give each child two magnets. Have a race to see who can "chase" the magnet across a desk first without ever touching the magnets together.

64. Plant Study (S. #3)

Materials needed: Seeds of all types—flowers, weeds, grasses, shrubs, trees, and so on.

Children really love activities that involve a competition of some sort. This one works well! Have students search, with the help of their parents, for the "Most Unusual Seed." They can also search for the "Largest" and/or "Smallest" seed possible. Students can either purchase one, such as a coconut (yes, the whole thing is a seed) or kiwi (itsy-bitsy), or locate seeds at home: dandelions, weeds, watermelon, corn, zinnias, peach pit, grass seed, and so on. In the classroom, have the children classify the seeds by color, size, edible/nonedible, useful/unwanted, and so forth.

This activity lends itself to a discussion about how seeds travel—for example, on animals and through the air. Children may also draw cross sections of different seeds or an illustration of various plant types such as bushes, trees, edible root plants, and vines. The classroom collection of seeds can be organized by gluing seeds on index cards with the name and type written on the backs of the cards.

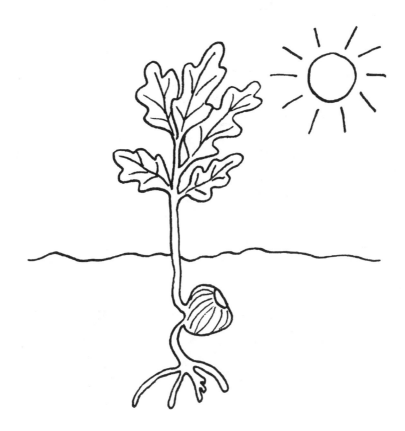

65. Wild Wacky Planets (S. #4)

Materials: Round coffee filters, washable markers, and spray bottle filled with water.

Have children use the markers to draw random colors or a colorful pattern on their filters. Once the filters are bright and colorful, spray the filters with water (an old tablecloth to work on is wise). The finished design will look rather "planetish." Mount the filters on black paper. With white or yellow crayon, children may draw in stars, rockets, and constellations.

For a creative writing project to accompany the "planet," have each child describe the planet's name, temperature, size, life forms, moons, atmosphere, and unusual features. In addition, a Venn diagram project could compare the imaginary planet's statistics with data on an existing planet. The children can develop speaking skills if they present to the class their data comparing real and imaginary planets.

66. Sea Scroll (S. #3)

Materials needed: Adding machine tape, art supplies, and enough scallop or similar shells for one per student.

After children have studied sea animals, this project makes an excellent take-home masterpiece. Cut a piece of adding machine tape 15 to 20 inches long for each child. Have the children fold the paper into eight equal sections and draw and label a sea creature that they are familiar with in each section. On the back, a sentence describing a characteristic of each creature should be placed in each of the eight spaces. When the children are done, roll the paper in a tube and tape it to one of the shells you've acquired. What a nice little "Sea Scroll" this makes!

The class could also tally all the different types of animals that children chose to illustrate and categorize them on the board by animal type: fish, mammal, arachnid, invertebrate, amphibian, and so on. A similar "scroll" could be made to share information on freshwater animal life. The freshwater "scroll" could be attached to a small twig.

Star Fish

67. Stuffed Animal Store (S.S. #7)

Materials needed: Stuffed animals (brought by students; see parent note in Figure 5.1), price tags, pencil, and sales slip (see Figure 5.2).

In social studies, a unit on economics is usually a high priority. Setting up a class store is a wonderful method of making the concept and terminology real to children. Make tags from $1.00 to $5.00 and have the children randomly select price tags for their animals. Attach the tags and put the animals in a store display. The children can be grouped to make advertising, window displays, and so forth. Give children $10.00 each in play money and have them take turns coming to the store to shop. They will have to make choices with their money and then help the "cashier" fill out the sales slip and figure their change. If desired, a sales tax percentage can be included in the calculations. The children would keep their new "friends" at their desks for a set time. By the end of the week, children will have a better understanding of consumers and retailers, goods and services, sales slips, credit cards, and banking.

Figure 5.1. Sample Parent Note

Dear Parents:

For the next couple of weeks, we are going to be exploring a social studies unit on economics. To help make the experience more meaningful, we are going to create a class store. I have asked the children to bring a stuffed animal from home that they are willing to share with the class for a week.

We are going to practice "buying" and "selling" the animals, so please make sure that the animal is a "friend" your child won't need for a while.

Thanks so much for your help.

Sincerely,

Figure 5.2. Sales Slip

SALES SLIP

Customer name: _____

Description of Items: *Purchase Price:*

_____   _____

_____   _____

_____   _____

_____   _____

_____   _____

Total for purchases: _____

Percentage sales tax: _____%

Tax cost: _____% × total = _____

Grand Total = Purchase + Tax Cost: _____

68. Cloud Book (S. #2)

Materials needed: Blue sentence strip paper, art supplies, and pencils.

Mentally connecting a scientific term with a common object is a great way to assist with memory of the terminology. The four basic types of clouds can easily be connected with common objects as follows: cirrus—feathers, cumulus—cauliflower, stratus—blanket, and fog—clouds all around us. Have children take a piece of blue sentence strip paper and fold it into fifths. In each section, they can write the type of cloud and the common object it resembles. On the back, they can draw a picture in each of the four sections and then use the fifth section to write, "My Cloud Book by _____." Have the children fold the book accordion style, and bravo—you've got those cloud types down. Sometime during the unit, try to take the class outside to observe actual examples of each cloud type.

69. Geography Pyramid (S.S. #3)

Materials needed: Tagboard and strips of sentence strip paper.

Children often don't have a clue when it comes to geographical terms and their relative size. This activity helps them figure their place in the universe. You will need a large drawing of a pyramid or, for the less artistic, a triangle divided in 10 sections horizontally from the bottom to the top. Label each section, starting at the bottom, with The Universe, My Planet, My Continent, My Country, My State, My City, My Neighborhood, My Street, My House, and Me. After that, the actual proper name of each can be placed on a separate sentence strip and placed over the original 10 categories, for example, Our Universe, Earth, North America, U.S.A., Virginia, Chesapeake, Crestwood, Hillwell Street, 228 Hillwell—me! It would be good to have each child create his or her personal "pyramid" for reference. With the visual illustration, children will understand much better the biggest to smallest idea of geographical terminology.

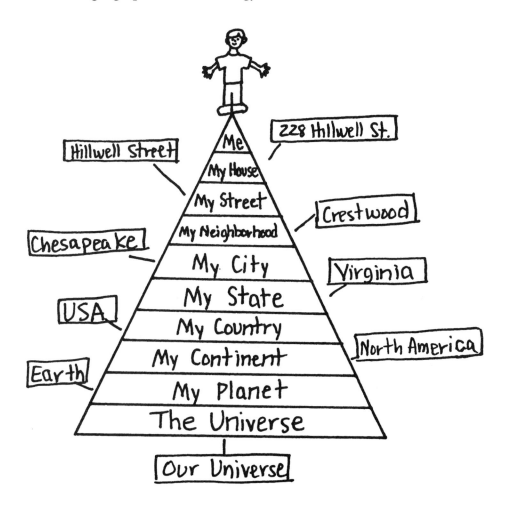

70. Soup Matters! (S. #1)

Materials needed: Five cups of broth frozen in a plastic container; a Crock-Pot; spoons; bowls; 1 cup each of cleaned, cut carrots, potatoes, celery; 1 can of tomatoes; half cup of barley; and 1 cup of pasta noodles.

Early in the morning, show all the students the frozen broth (example of a solid). Note with the class how it retains its shape when taken out of the container. Put the frozen broth in the Crock-Pot and turn it on high for an hour. Have the children observe that the broth is now melted (turned into a liquid). They will see that the liquid takes the shape of whatever container it's in. At this point, add the fresh vegetables and the barley. A few spices may be added for flavor. Next, let the mixture cook for 2 to 3 hours. By early afternoon, the liquid should be quite hot, and steam (gas) will rise when the lid is lifted. Have the children note that the gas spreads throughout the room and has no shape. Stir in the pasta and cook for another half hour. Then it's chow time! What a great way to learn changes of state!

6

Seasonal Ideas

The ideas in this section are arranged by month in order throughout the school year from September through June. For each month of the school year, there is one activity that involves artwork, poetry, cultural awareness, scientific exploration, or other educational concepts. These ideas are alternatives to the typical construction paper/pattern art projects that have been used for years. Many of them can be adjusted to meet mandatory school curriculum standards so they need not be considered just "fluff" added for fun. Regardless of the content, the children will enjoy these projects, and the parents will appreciate the results when they come home.

71. September: Calendar Creation (M. #2)

Materials needed: Blank calendar sheets with space for illustrations at the top, art supplies, pencils, and pens.

Creating calendars is a good project to initiate shortly after school starts. The goal is to have an original calendar (for the next year) created by each child. If you start early, you will be finished by winter break. For each month, discuss with the class how many days are in each month, what day the month starts and ends on, how to spell the name of the month, special events that occur during the month, and so on. Then, give children one blank calendar sheet each and have them put in the appropriate dates and special events. The children will also illustrate each month with a picture that represents their vision of what happens during that month. By doing one calendar page per week, for 12 weeks, by December your class should have 12 pages for 12 months. Children can then design covers. Once calendars are bound, they make excellent parent gifts.

72. October: Descriptive Writing/Poetry (L.A. #5)

Materials needed: Paper, pencils, and imagination.

This language/poetry activity is a good one to work on in October. The main language content covered is descriptive language, synonyms, and parts of speech. Follow this pattern:

Ghost	A single noun
White, eerie	Two adjectives
Swirling, screeching, haunting	Three verbs
The spirit floats along	A four-word phrase
SPOOK!!!	A synonym to the original word

A good idea is to have the poem take the shape of the topic chosen, such as a ghost or pumpkin. Other possible October topics are witch/banshee, pumpkin/jack-o'-lantern, cat/feline, moon/golden orb, vampire/Dracula, and ghoul/beast. Here's another chance for great illustrations and playing "Around the World" (see Idea 45) with synonyms.

73. November: Indian Study/Tepees (S.S. #5)

> **Materials needed:** Soft shells for tacos, markers and/or food coloring, Q-tips, toothpicks, 1 tub chocolate frosting, and stick pretzels.

Taco shell tepees are fun for the children to make and can be used to teach about symbols used by Indians in art and clothing and about Indian homes for migratory tribes. First, have the children decorate the circular shells with the markers or food coloring applied with Q-tips. The decorating should follow content about Indian symbols. Next, have the children fold the shell into a cone shape and secure it with toothpicks. The pretzels will appear to be the tepee poles if "glued" with chocolate frosting. Each tepee could be set on a tagboard square, and children may add natural and environmental features such as a campfire (twigs, paper flames, and rocks), trees (small pine pieces), and Indian and animal paper cutouts. A good use for the rest of the frosting and pretzels is to write (in an Indian alphabet) each child's name. Other types of Indian homes, such as the pueblo and the longhouse, could be discussed as well.

74. December: Create and Celebrate Day (M. #9)

Materials needed: Have students ask their parents for these: glitter; colored glue (food coloring in household glue works); tagboard cutouts of Santa, trees, bells, and so on; cardboard egg cartons cut into individual sections; old Christmas cards; candy canes; ribbon; sequins; yarn; colored tissue; pinecones; and any other artsy materials you can find!

An annual tradition that children love is a "Create and Celebrate" afternoon close to the time for winter break. Because this is a hectic time, parent volunteers are essential to help ensure success. The idea is for the children to rotate among a number of centers and create tree decorations. Children may choose to make easy ornaments such as these:

1. Add a string to a pinecone and decorate with glue, sequins, and glitter.

2. Take a candy cane, add twisted pipe cleaners for antlers and jiggle eyes—what a reindeer!

3. A tagboard cutout with a hole punched at the top and ribbon and decorations added can become a "masterpiece" for a young child.

4. Egg carton sections can become bells when a string, craft bell, and glitter are added.

5. Christmas cards make wonderful miniature gift boxes. Have children follow these directions: Cut the card apart at fold. Fold in middle vertically and horizontally (teach the terminology). Fold once more from each side to create 16 equal sections (see Figure 6.1). Do this with both front and back of card. Cut out the four corner sections from each. One piece creates the top of the box and the other creates the bottom. Add a ribbon to the box and put it on the tree.

6. Tree shapes will become three-dimensional when small bits of tissue are molded over the end of a pencil and then glued in place all over the tree.

Display ornaments in the hallway by taking sticky tack and attaching ribbon to create a tree shape —a simple triangle looks nice. Add a trunk and then sticky tack ornaments on the "tree." You will get many compliments!

Figure 6.1. Folding a Card to Make Miniature Gift Box

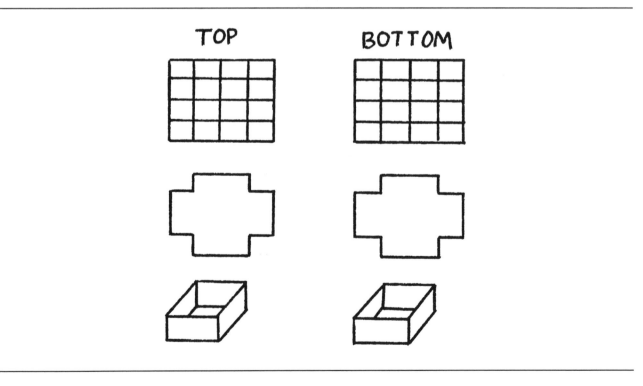

75. January: New Year's Resolutions (L.A. #4)

Materials needed: Paper and pencils.

The beginning of the year is a good time for children to assess their goals. A fun way to do that is to write resolutions. Duplicate the following sentences:

In _____, I resolve to learn about _____.

I also want to be better at _____.

I predict that the following will happen this year: _____.

Signed by _____ on this _____ day of _____.

Use the sheets to make a New Year's display, then bind all the sheets together in a "Resolutions" book. Near the end of the school year, have the children look at the resolutions and either orally or through a written essay describe how well they have accomplished their personal goals.

76. February: Silly Valentine Puns (L.A. #12)

Materials needed: Samples of children's valentines, art supplies, and paper.

Students in the elementary grades get a great deal of pleasure from giving and receiving valentines. The more you put that interest to use in an educational way, the more you'll hold your students' interest. Many valentines use puns or plays on words to get their message across. Put the following valentine phrases on the board for children to discuss what animal or topic the phrases are referring to.

You're Fetching!	(dog)
It Would Be Tweet If You'd Be Mine!	(bird)
I Like You Beary Much!	(bear)
You're Purrr-fectly Wonderful!	(cat)
I'm on a Roll When You're Around!	(roller skates)
Hope Your Valentine's Day Is Tutu Fun!	(ballerina)

A discussion of contractions could be slipped in almost unnoticed. Afterward, the children could each create a valentine (to give to someone special) with an original play on words.

77. March: Signs of Spring Mobile (S. #6)

Materials needed: Poster paper, stencils for geometric shapes, tagboard, yarn, coat hangers, and art supplies.

A fun project as the weather starts looking springlike is the Signs of Spring Mobile. To introduce this project, take a nature walk around the school grounds while students try to spot indications that spring is near, such as grass turning green, birds chirping, rain falling, lighter jackets being worn, and so on. After the walk, hold a class discussion about all the indicators of spring that the children have found. Compile all the ideas in a poster titled "The Many, Varied, and Unusual Signs That Spring Is Near."

Have the children make individual or team Signs of Spring Mobiles that show pictures or phrases describing spring. Provide stencils in sign shapes, such as triangles, circles, rectangles, and squares. Here's an excellent opportunity for a little geometry review and/or traffic sign introduction. Have children attach the illustrated shapes to hangers with pieces of yarn. Yeah, Spring!

78. April: Letter Writing/Teacher Appreciation (L.A. #5)

Materials needed: Paper and pencils.

Typically, April is the month when local parent-teacher associations host a Teacher Appreciation Week. Most classroom teachers receive numerous warm fuzzies during that time, and morale is boosted. Unfortunately, the resource teachers (e.g., P.E., art, library, and guidance) are usually neglected during this time. An excellent writing assignment is to have children choose resource teachers they are fond of and have them write letters telling the teachers what they appreciate about them. This project provides a purpose for writing letters and also a wonderful and most appreciated surprise for important members of the staff.

Another teacher appreciation project is a book about the special people in school. Assign each child a resource teacher, principal, secretary, janitor, or other staff member. Have each child discuss the staff person's responsibilities and create a picture with a few sentences telling why that person is important.

79. May: Camping/Oral Story Time (L.A. #4)

Materials needed: Chocolate candies, crunchy square cereal, pretzels, marshmallows, sunflower seeds, raisins, and other dried fruit; large mixing bowl and spoon; and napkins, bowls, and spoons.

As the days warm up, children start to think about summer adventures to come. Many children have gone camping (or most certainly would like to go camping), so a good reward activity is to make a special trail mix and share camping or scary stories. A week or so before the scheduled event, send a note to the students' parents asking for the materials listed above (see Figure 6.2). With the help of your students, take the food items (they could be weighed for measurement practice) and mix them together in a large bowl. The children will have a blast eating a bowl of the mix somewhere pleasant on the school grounds and telling imaginary tales of terror (acceptable limits set, of course). Stimulate creativity by making up imaginary settings such as, "Joe, remember this morning when you and I were fishing and we heard a growl coming out of the forest . . ?" Later, the stories could be written to share with families. Discuss with the children the idea of oral tradition and how folktales have been passed down from generation to generation.

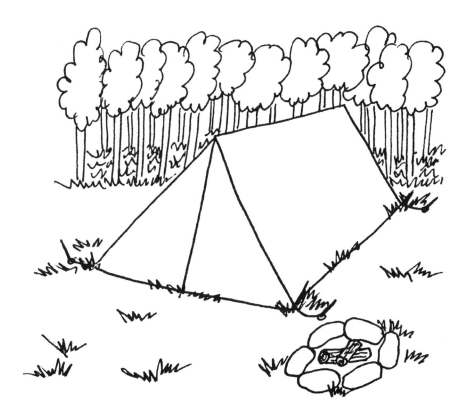

Figure 6.2. Sample Parent Note Requesting Materials

Dear Parents,

On _____, our class is going to have a special storytelling and snacking time. We are going to pretend to be camping and share stories around the "campfire." For this to be successful, we need your help. Please send in one of the items listed so that we can mix it together and create trail mix. Materials needed include chocolate candies, marshmallows, sunflower seeds, crunchy square cereal, pretzels, raisins, and dried fruit. Also, we need paper napkins, bowls, and plastic spoons.

Thanks!

---

80. June: Autograph/Memory Book (L.A. #4)

Materials needed: For each student, an 8- to 10-page packet of loose-leaf paper stapled in book form, pencils, markers, and so on.

The end of the year is a happy time, but it can also be sentimental. The children love to have special mementos to remember their classmates and teacher. A Trivia Autograph Book is a nice way to preserve their memories. The front page will consist of a class list. Each child (and you, the teacher, too!) chooses a number for a code number, for example, Tara—#456 and Carter—#1. Each of the other pages will have a question such as, What is your favorite sport? Food? Pet? Memory from this year? Place to go? Have the children sit in a circle and pass the books one space at a time clockwise. The students end up answering questions in everyone else's book.

Example: What is your favorite sport? Tennis—456 (Tara likes tennis).

The class continues to pass the books around the circle until all students have answered in everyone's book. Years later, some children will still have their books!

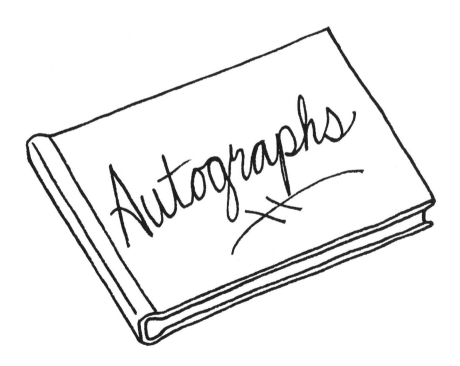

7

Fun Activities for Outdoor or Active Play

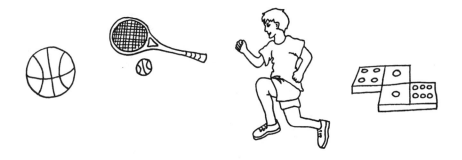

The activities in this section are quick to prepare with few materials needed. They are perfect to consider when planning an end-of-the-year party or other celebration. They can also be used to provide structure to recess time. These games and races will be enjoyed by children and will contribute to physical fitness at the same time.

81. "Horsey" Riding Relay

Materials needed: Two pool "noodles" and two hats (western, preferably).

Divide the class into two teams. The goal for team members is to ride the noodle in horseback fashion to a predetermined spot while wearing the hat. If a child gets "bucked off" the horse or loses the hat, the child must start over. When the riders get back to their team, they can yell "Go, Buckaroo!" and then the next player starts. The first team done is the champ. Yee-haw!

82. Clothes Basket Catch

Materials needed: Two clothes baskets and as many tennis balls as you can acquire. (Tennis clubs will donate old balls if asked.)

Divide the group in two. The goal is to get the tennis ball into the basket. At the beginning, the children will simply throw the ball into the basket from a set point. Later, have two children hold the basket on their head and tilt or lift to try to catch the balls as the team members are tossing them. Other variations could be only overhand throws, underhand throws, and so forth. The team with the most balls in the basket after everyone has had three or four tries is the winner.

A similar game can be used in the classroom to review concepts. For this, get a small wall-mounted basketball hoop and foam ball. Divide the class in two and ask questions (say, on astronomy or ancient Egypt). The first team who gets the right answer gets a chance to make a basket. Keep score and reward the team that has the most points at the end of the review. The children will be listening!

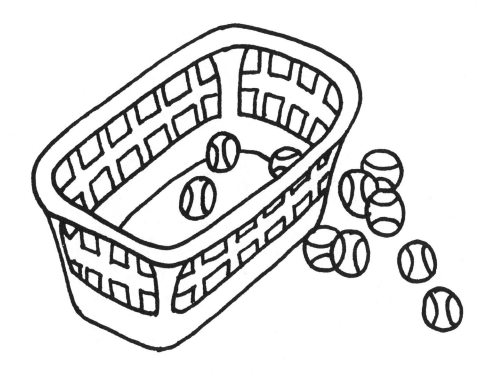

83. Circle Ball Toss

Material needed: Soft playground ball.

Have the group of children stand in a circle with their legs spread so that their feet are touching those of the children on either side. One student is in the center with the ball. The goal is to get the ball through the legs of someone in the circle. Legs cannot move, but the ball may be stopped by the hands. If the ball gets through a child's legs, the child is out. Occasionally, pick a new center person. As the players get out, the circle will get smaller and smaller until you're down to one. This simple game could evolve into various measurement activities:

1. Find the center of the circle and measure the radius and diameter.
2. Discuss and measure the circumference (perimeter) of the circle.
3. See who in the class can stretch the farthest and measure his or her leg span.
4. Count how many times a student can throw the ball in a minute (TPM—throws per minute—versus MPH—miles per hour).
5. Use the figures above plus students' learned knowledge to determine the area of the circle.

Ah, the line between recreation and learning is blurred again!

84. Newspaper Race

Materials needed: Individual sections from the newspaper.

The goal of this game is to get from point A to point B by stepping only on newspaper. Divide the group into two teams. Each contestant is given only two pieces of paper. The process involves stepping on one paper and then placing the second piece in front and stepping on it. After that, the piece from behind has to be moved from behind and the person steps forward. The process continues until everyone reaches the finish line, and then one by one each does the same thing back. Lots of stretching will occur without the children's awareness. While the children are waiting for their turn, have them read their section of the newspaper (preselect the reading materials). When everyone is done, discuss as a class current events, the punch line of a comic strip, advice given by a columnist, or what to watch on television that night.

85. Who's Leading?

Materials needed: None.

This game is a great choice when a break is needed in the classroom routine. Choose one student to be the detective who will try to find the "leading" person. The detective needs to wait in the hall while you organize the group. Get the children into a circle and choose one leader. The leader's job is to start any motion he or she chooses. Examples include blinking eyes, waving arms over head, lifting knees, marching, wiggling nose, and so on. When the detective enters the room, the entire group will be doing the leader's chosen motion. As the game progresses, the leader slyly switches to other movements (the other students should follow suit as quickly as possible). The detective's task is to identify the leader with the fewest guesses possible. Occasionally, choose a new detective and leader. The creative children will stand out with their imaginative motions of choice.

86. Rescue Relay

Materials needed: Tape for finish line.

Divide the class into two equal groups. Mark a finish line approximately 25 feet away. One member of each team starts at the finish line and runs to the team. The runner grabs the first member of his or her team by the hand, and they both run back to the finish line. Then, the second player runs back to the team (the first stays put) and grabs the hand of the next team member. Runners go back and forth until all team members have been rescued.

A more challenging version of the game is to pick two "sharks" to be on their bellies in the water. Their challenge is to try to slither quickly and touch the feet of a team member. If touched, those team members are out. Play continues until only one team has runners left. If the sharks aren't very successful, then add "piranhas," "eels," or other sea creatures. Check for great teamwork in your class. This could provide a fun break when students are working hard on a sea creature unit—or for fun, try it with animals of the forest, desert, or polar region.

87. Domino Relay

Materials needed: Enough domino blocks for four per child.

Divide the class into two teams. The first person from each team runs to the counter with their four dominoes and sets them upright on the counter. They run back and tag the next team member, who runs forward and does the same thing. Suggest that students line the dominoes up in a snakelike shape. This continues until all members of each team have placed their dominoes upright. If they bump one or more of the dominoes while putting up their own, they must set them back up as well. The team finished setting up first gets a 10-point bonus. The teacher then touches each "snake" to start the domino effect. Each domino that falls counts as one point. The team with the most points wins. (A discussion of chain reactions would be great!) When the game is over, initiate a contest in which each team adds the total of dots on all their dominoes. The team with the quickest finish or largest total wins.

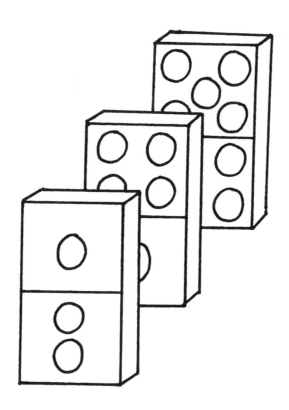

88. Bubble Gum Circle

Materials needed: Bubble gum.

This activity can easily be done in the classroom. Give one piece of gum to each child. Divide the group into two teams. Each team makes a circle standing and facing each other. When you say "Go!" everyone tries to blow a bubble. Each person sits after blowing a bubble. The team that gets three fourths of its members seated first wins. (This is a great opportunity to figure out how many three fourths would be—fractions in everyday life.) A variation of this activity could be largest bubble contest, bubbles inside of bubbles, and so on.

Using a bubble as a prop, you could also remind the children that gases are real and can be confined to a space. To further make that concept clear, blow up and knot a balloon to show how the balloon takes up space and contains a gas (invisible but real). Also, show how gases can exert a force by blowing up and releasing a balloon. Children can watch it fly and flip through the air (forced air propellent).

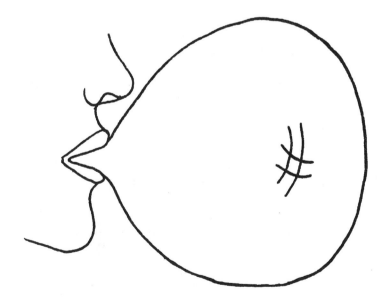

89. Obstacle Race Relay

Materials needed: Chairs and two blankets to create two tunnels, two boxes, more chairs, paper to make two balls, and two trash cans.

The three obstacles in the race are the box hurdle to jump, the chair-blanket tunnel to crawl through, and the five-chair path to run through. The course ends with the trash can goal in which to toss a paper ball. Divide the class into two teams. Each child starts with a wad of paper. The team members go through each obstacle as quickly as possible and then throw the paper wad into the trash can. They then run back to the next member of their team, who will do the same thing. Members of the team that finishes first are the "Obstacle Pros!" Yippee!

To encourage teamwork and creativity, give the same materials to half of the class and see what type of obstacle course the children create for the rest of the class to go through. Of course, students in the other half would have to try their hand, too. This is a fun activity to turn the kids loose on during a day before a break!

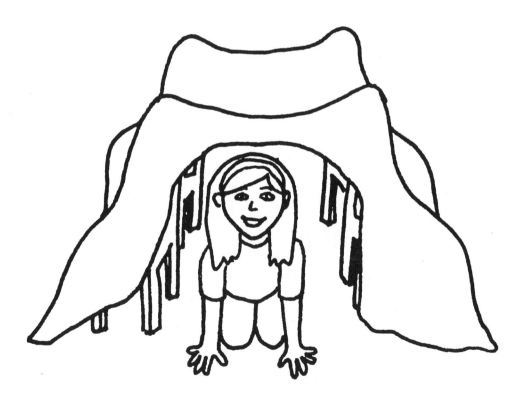

90. Frisbee Team Toss

Materials needed: Two frisbees and construction paper.

Divide the group into two teams. Take various colors of construction paper and put point values on them (5 points to 100 points). Place the papers randomly around the area. Each team member takes turns tossing the frisbee, trying to make it land on the papers on the floor. Once one has been hit, you (or designated student) will gather the paper off the floor and give it to the team that hit it. When all team members have had a couple of chances, have the teams work together to add up their points to see who won. (This activity is great for silly fun and addition practice!) The class could also try the same activity with paper airplanes that they've created. First, study the principles of aerodynamics and see who should plan to be a future aviation engineer!

91. Sponge Squeeze

Materials needed: Two empty liter soda bottles, two sponges, and two buckets of water.

Divide the group into two teams. The goal for team members is to take the saturated sponge out of the bucket, run to the liter bottle, and squeeze as much water as possible into it. The first team with a full bottle wins. By the end of the fun, the children will have an accurate understanding of a liter.

In addition, children can measure the amount of water in one saturated sponge in milliliters and then figure out how many trips it should take to fill the liter bottle (milliliter-liter comparison). They could also count how many children/trips it did take to fill the liter bottle and calculate the approximate waste per trip. This is a good choice for a grade-level field day activity.

For a comparison of liters and quarts, have the teams try the same process with a quart container to see which takes longer to fill, a liter or a quart. After this experience, the children will be able to differentiate between the metric and nonmetric systems of measurement.

92. Leaky Milk Jug Race

Materials needed: Two milk jugs (cut open at top and with 20+ holes poked into each) and two large containers of water (garbage cans, big buckets, etc.).

The day before this activity, tell the children that they should wear clothes that dry quickly. Divide the group into two teams. The goal is to empty the large container of water by scooping with the leaky milk jug and passing it overhead to the child behind. The jug moves over the team members' heads until it gets to the end. The last person runs to the front, and the process starts again. Play continues until the container is empty and all are wet, wet, wet!

For a less messy variation, have team members scoop and run to a liter bottle that each team fills. Obviously, this activity should take place outside when the weather is warm—perhaps in conjunction with some celebration such as the end of the school year.

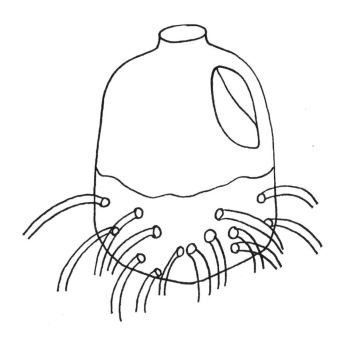

93. Water Balloon Toss

Materials needed: One beach towel or blanket per four children and one or two water balloons per child.

Divide the group into groups of four (have the children note the division) with each child holding a corner of his or her team's beach towel or blanket. The goal is to see how long the groups can bounce their water balloons into the air without breaking them. The groups really have to work together. Once they have gotten the hang of it, they can try to toss the balloons from group to group. (This activity can also be done with two sheets and half of the class spread around each sheet.) Afterward, hold a discussion of strategies.

If you are a brave teacher who is anxious to really excite your students, volunteer to be the target in a "Throw the Water Balloon at the Teacher Game." Your students will remember you as the most fun teacher ever!

94. Pantomime Power

Materials needed: None.

Type the ideas shown in Figure 7.1 on small slips of paper. Have the children act out the ideas without any speaking or props. (This is a great opportunity to assess theatrical abilities and nonverbal communication skills.)

Figure 7.1. Pantomime Ideas

Brushing Teeth	Playing Tennis
Making a Bed	Fixing a Flat Tire
Playing the Piano	Painting Fingernails
Washing the Car	Fixing a Salad
Loading the Dishwasher	Putting a Key in the Door
Planting a Flower	Skipping Rope
Drinking Coffee	Having a Nightmare
Reading the Paper	

8
Motivational and Organizational Ideas

Organization and having a bag of "tricks" are among the most important elements of successful teaching. The less downtime you have during the day, the more the children will learn, the less discipline problems you will have, and the more the children will respect and like you. I'm sure that sounds good to all educators!

One of the best ways to prevent discipline problems is to have good rules. The rules need to be clear and easily understood. The children will take more ownership of rules if they help in the formation of the rules at the beginning of the year. Four to five rules are the maximum needed. In addition to establishing rules, make sure that the children know the consequences for repeated breaking of the rules. The goal is to have the majority of your concern not on how to control but rather on how to motivate and excite.

95. Funny Money

Materials needed: Teacher-created slips of paper "money"—lots of them.

To motivate and reward students for excellent academic achievement or behavior, your own "currency" is effective. The name of the currency should relate to the teacher, for example, "Dodson's Dollars," "Brock's Bucks," and "Moseley's Money." At the beginning of the year, explain that the dollars will be given out for perfect tests, extra effort on projects, examples of kind and helpful behavior, good citizenship, and other positive actions observed in the classroom. When children collect "$20," they may go "shopping" in a special prize box or receive another incentive that you come up with. (You can even offer extraspecial treats such as sitting at the teacher's desk for the day.) The children should be held responsible for putting their names on the money so that no one could gain from stealing. Children love and are motivated by this activity.

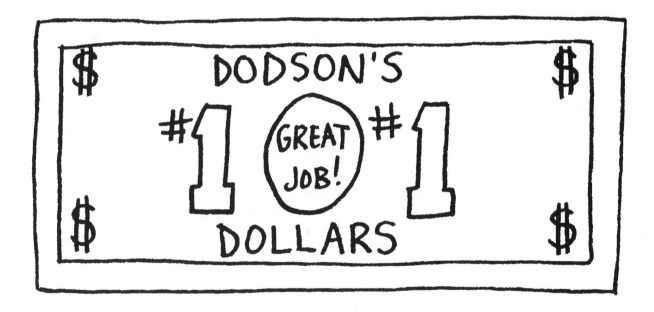

96. Class Prize Bag

Materials needed: Happy Meal and similar toys, dollar-store goodies, junk jewelry, baseball cards, sticker sets, and other small items currently collected by the children.

Children today are accustomed to receiving some sort of prize almost daily. Having rewards ready for extraspecial accomplishments is an effective technique to use for motivation. One way to successfully deal with prizes is to acquire a big Prize Bag or class Treasure Chest. At the beginning of the year, tell your students' parents that you are putting together a prize bag and would appreciate their help. Ask for gently used Happy Meal prizes. You can also request dollar-store items. If you have created your own currency (see Idea 95), you will be amazed at how hard the students will work to gather their $20. Occasionally, when the selections are getting rather picked over, hold an auction in which children can bid on a prize.

Example: Who will offer me $1 for this fine car? $2? . . .

This is motivating to the child who just can't collect $20!

97. Floor Patrol

Materials needed: A willingness to be helpful.

Does the janitor complain about your classroom cleanup? You will have no more complaints if you explain to your students that each day you'll need "Floor Patrol" volunteers to manually pick up all scraps and other assorted garbage off the floor. Be sure to have the children clean their hands after the task is finished. You can reward those students who generously volunteer frequently (see Idea 95). If this activity is presented in a positive light, you will be amazed at how the children jump at the opportunity to clean. Wouldn't it be refreshing if that happened at home, too! When complimenting your students on their helpfulness, extend the discussion by making a "Ways We Help" chart. Maybe those less-than-motivated types will get the hint that it's about time they do their part!

98. Freeze!

Materials needed: Flexible bodies and good balance.

Many times, group activities and fun and games in the classroom can start to get out of order. A simple, fast way to regain control of your class is the "freeze" technique. Explain to students that when you say "Freeze!" they are to freeze exactly where they are and listen for instructions. Instruct them to hold their pose just like statues, and say that you will be watching for the best "freezers." The children are to remain frozen until you say "Unfreeze!" You can keep order easily with this simple approach that children enjoy.

For a fun art activity related to "Freeze," have children form human body shapes out of clay, duplicating some of the interesting poses the children have seen around them. This would be a natural time to discuss human muscle and bone structure. Maybe you have a future Michelangelo!

99. Class Magnets

Materials needed: Tagboard child shapes (boy and girl), art supplies, and strips of sticky magnet.

At the beginning of the school year, give each child a blank "Kid Shape" to draw and color with their attributes. There needs to be space on each for the child's name as well. This activity will give you a good idea of individual artistic abilities, manual dexterity, and some self-concept input. Laminate and attach a magnet to each of the "kids." The resulting magnets can be used in many ways: keeping track of lunch choices, creating bar graphs on favorites and personal data, noting students who are finished with tasks, assigning groups, and so forth. Also, at the end of the year, the kid shapes make nice mementos!

100. School Supply Buckets

Materials needed: Plastic buckets or snack canisters.

I'm sure that every teacher has been frustrated by students who do not have the necessary supplies in their desks. A simple trick that helps with this problem is to keep supplies in large buckets or canisters near your desk and pass out the supplies only as the need arises. Some supplies to stockpile in this fashion are pencils (request 25 at the beginning and pass out as needed), glue (no more in-the-desk spills), markers and colored pencils (they can be used for group projects, and no more students will be sad because they don't have any), and even crayons (they can be grouped so that there is a "bucket" for each table when needed). This technique makes resources much more equal in the classroom for the haves and the have-nots.

101. Class Bear

> **Materials needed:** A large stuffed animal (bear, bunny, etc.) and a journal for writing about experiences.

At the beginning of the school year, bring in a large stuffed animal that you have acquired via a garage sale or other inexpensive fashion. This animal becomes a class mascot. Have the class vote on a name for the animal (a good time to teach about nominations and use of ballots). Each Friday, pick a name out of a jar and send the Class Bear home with a student for the weekend. A journal goes with the bear. Each "baby-sitter" must write an entry about her or his experience with the bear to share with the class on Monday. The journal entry could be an imaginary adventure, such as "Sweetie Bear's Trip to Mars," or something realistic, such as "Our Trip to the Grocery Store." This activity encourages creativity and family involvement. For a special reward in the classroom, select children to sit with, read with, or rock with the class bear. Children of all ages and genders are receptive to a cuddle time.

Index

CORWIN
PRESS

The Corwin Press logo—a raven striding across an open book—represents the happy union of courage and learning. We area professional-level publisher of books and journals for K-12 educators, and we are committed to creating and providing resources that embody these qualities. Corwin's motto is "Success for All Learners."